WAR PLANES

Long-Range Bombers:
The B-1B Lancers

by Michael and Gladys Green

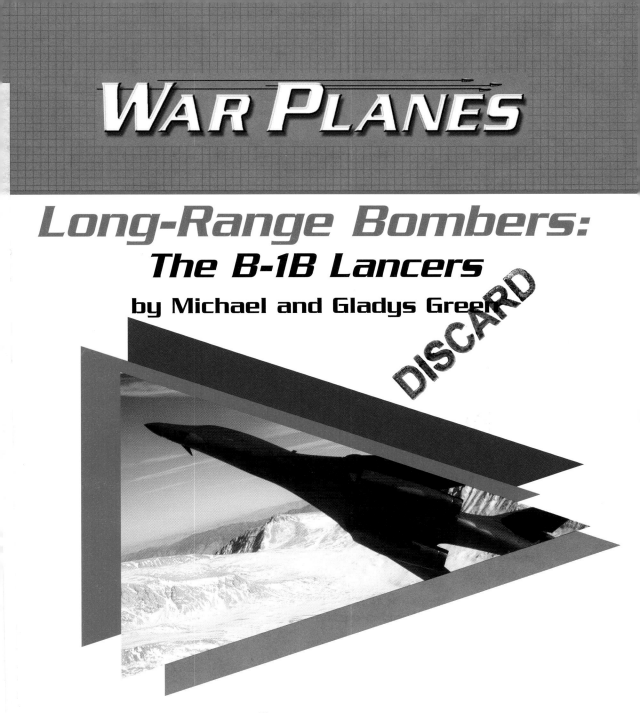

CAPSTONE
HIGH-INTEREST
BOOKS

an imprint of Capstone Press
Mankato, Minnesota

Capstone High-Interest Books are published by Capstone Press
151 Good Counsel Drive, P.O. Box 669, Mankato, Minnesota 56002
http://www.capstone-press.com

Library of Congress Cataloging-in-Publication Data
Green, Michael, 1952–
    Long-range bombers: the B-1B Lancers/by Michael and Gladys Green.
    p. cm.—(War planes)
    Summary: Introduces the B-1B Lancers, their specifications, equipment,
weapons, missions, and future in the Air Force.
    Includes bibliographical references and index.
    ISBN 0-7368-1508-2 (hardcover)
    1. B-1 bomber—Juvenile literature. [1. B-1 bomber. 2. Bombers.] I. Green,
Gladys, 1954– II. Title. III. Series.
UG1242.B6 G72 2003
623.7'463—dc21   2002007926

Editorial Credits
Carrie Braulick, editor; Eric Kudalis, product planning editor; Timothy Halldin,
    series designer; Gene Bentdahl and Molly Nei, book designers; Jo Miller,
    photo researcher

Photo Credits
Defense Visual Information Center, 1, 8 (all), 12 (all), 14 (all), 16, 22, 25, 28
Photo by Ted Carlson/Fotodynamics, cover, 4, 7, 9, 10, 13, 18–19, 20
Photri-Microstock, 26

**Special thanks to Michelle M. Weiss, Air Combat Command Public Affairs
Office, for her assistance in preparing this book.**

1 2 3 4 5 6 08 07 06 05 04 03

Table of Contents

Chapter One

Learn About

➤ **B-1B development**
➤ **B-1B design**
➤ **Radar systems**

The B-1B in Action

A U.S. Air Force B-1B Lancer flies over an enemy country at night. The B-1B's crew locates its target. Doors at the bottom of the aircraft open, and a large bomb drops from the plane. As the bomb explodes, it launches hundreds of smaller bombs. An enemy missile base is destroyed.

Enemy radar systems locate the bomber. One enemy missile flies toward the B-1B. A computer in the B-1B releases a decoy that is towed behind the aircraft. The decoy confuses the missile's guidance system and the missile misses the bomber.

An enemy pilot then fires a heat-seeking guided missile at the B-1B. The B-1B launches bright, hot flares. The missile follows the flares instead of the bomber. The B-1B crew returns safely to a nearby air base.

Building the B-1B

In 1965, the Air Force wanted a new long-range bomber to replace its outdated B-52 Stratofortress bombers. In 1974, aircraft manufacturer Rockwell International completed a test model of a new bomber. The Air Force ordered 240 final models. These planes were called B-1As. But the B-1As were never built. Government officials canceled the project in 1977. They did not believe the planes were needed.

In 1981, government officials once again approved the program. Rockwell International soon built an improved model of the B-1A called the B-1B. The Air Force ordered

The Air Force has more than 70 B-1Bs in service.

more than 100 B-1Bs. In 1985, the
Air Force received its first model. Today,
the Air Force flies more than 70 B-1Bs.

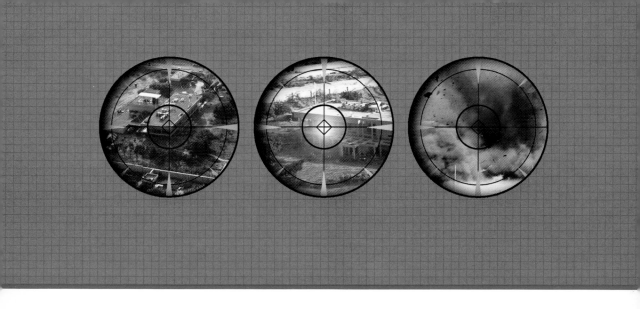

About the B-1B

The Air Force depends on B-1B crews to perform missions anywhere in the world on short notice. The B-1B is designed to travel long distances to reach a target. It is one of the Air Force's fastest bombers. It also is capable of carrying a great deal of weapons.

Pilots often fly the B-1B low to the ground during missions. Enemy radar systems cannot easily detect planes flying close to the ground.

The B-1B has features to help crew members perform their missions. A defensive countermeasures system protects the aircraft from enemy weapons. Radar equipment helps crew members aim weapons and keep track of their surroundings.

The B-1B is one of the Air Force's fastest bombers.

Chapter Two

Learn About

- VG wings
- Countermeasures system
- Flying the B-1B

Inside the B-1B

The B-1B can weigh up to 477,000 pounds (216,634 kilograms) when loaded with weapons and equipment. It has the largest payload of any Air Force bomber. The B-1B has a sturdy frame and strong landing gear to handle the weight.

The B-1B must carry a large payload over long distances. Tankers can refuel the plane during flight. The B-1B crew then can continue to fly instead of landing to refuel.

Adjustable Wings

The wings of most planes do not move. But the B-1B's wings can move forward or backward. They are called variable geometry (VG) wings. For takeoffs and landings, B-1B pilots point the wings straight out. This position helps the aircraft quickly climb and fall.

Pilots often point the wings toward the tail during flight. This wing position reduces drag. Drag occurs when air strikes a moving object. It slows down planes as they fly. The B-1B can fly faster with its wings swept back than it can with the wings straight out.

Powerful Engines

Four large jet engines power the B-1B. Each engine can produce about 30,000 pounds

The jet engines on the B-1B help it travel quickly.

(13,600 kilograms) of thrust. This force pushes
the aircraft through the air.

The B-1B's engines give it a top speed
of more than 900 miles (1,448 kilometers)
per hour. But B-1B pilots usually fly about
550 miles (900 kilometers) per hour to save fuel.

Countermeasures System

The AN/ALQ-161A countermeasures system protects the B-1B from enemy weapons. It warns the crew if radar-directed missiles approach the plane's rear. It may send out a towed decoy that confuses the missile's guidance system. The missile then flies between the plane and the decoy instead of hitting the plane. The AN/ALQ-161A's radar jammer also can send out electronic signals to prevent enemy radar systems from working properly.

The AN/ALQ-161A sometimes releases strips of metal called chaff. Each metal strip reflects radar energy to the station to confuse the radar system.

B-1B Specifications

Function:	Long-range bomber
Manufacturer:	Rockwell International/Boeing
Date Deployed:	1985
Length:	146 feet (44.5 meters)
Wingspan:	137 feet (41.8 meters) with wings extended forward
	79 feet (24.1 meters) with wings folded backward
Height:	34 feet (10.4 meters)
Weight:	477,000 pounds (216,634 kilograms)
Payload:	75,000 pounds (34,020 kilograms)
Engine:	Four General Electric F101-GE-102 jet engines
Speed:	900 miles (1,448 kilometers) per hour
Range:	7,500 miles (12,070 kilometers); unlimited with in-flight refueling

The AN/ALQ-161A can send out flares. The flares help protect the B-1B from heat-seeking missiles. These missiles are designed to follow a plane's hot engine exhaust. The missiles may follow the flares instead of the plane's exhaust.

The SMCS keeps the B-1B level during flight.

Navigational and Control Systems

Pilots fly the B-1B at fast speeds close to the ground. The aircraft could easily crash into the ground or other objects. The B-1B has an autopilot system to help pilots fly low. A computer is connected to a terrain-following radar (TFR) system in the aircraft's nose. Pilots look at the cockpit's radar screen to see objects in their flight path. The computer automatically flies the aircraft around the objects.

Air currents close to the ground can make the B-1B's ride bumpy. The B-1B has a Structural Mode Control System (SMCS). Two small wings called vanes are located in front of the plane's cockpit. The vanes are connected to a computer. The computer detects rough air and adjusts the vanes to keep the plane level.

B-1B Crew

Four crew members fly in the B-1B. The pilot and mission commander sit at the front of the cockpit. They operate the control systems to fly the plane.

The offensive systems operator (OSO) and defensive systems operator (DSO) sit in the rear of the cockpit. The OSO uses the plane's radar system to aim and release weapons. The DSO controls the B-1B's countermeasures system.

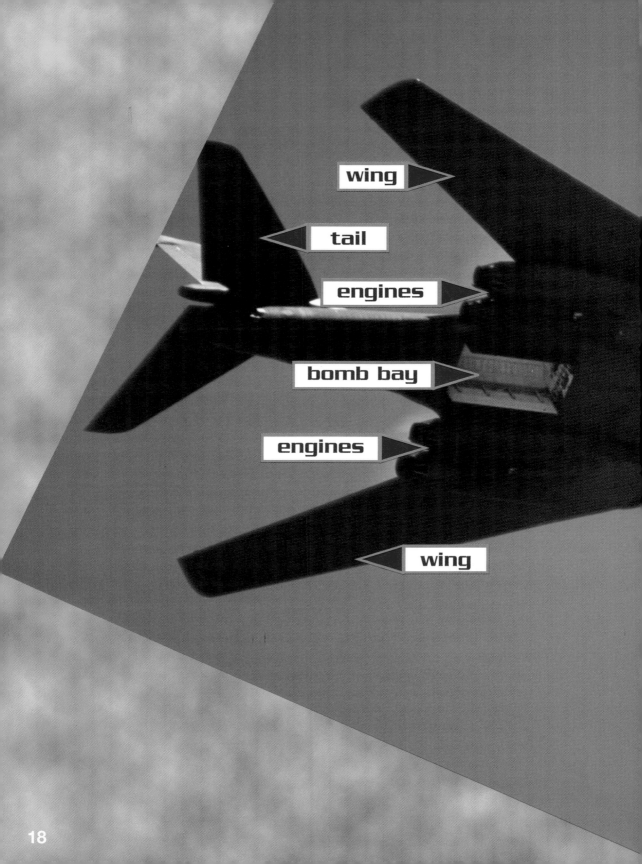

wing

tail

engines

bomb bay

engines

wing

The B-1B Bomber

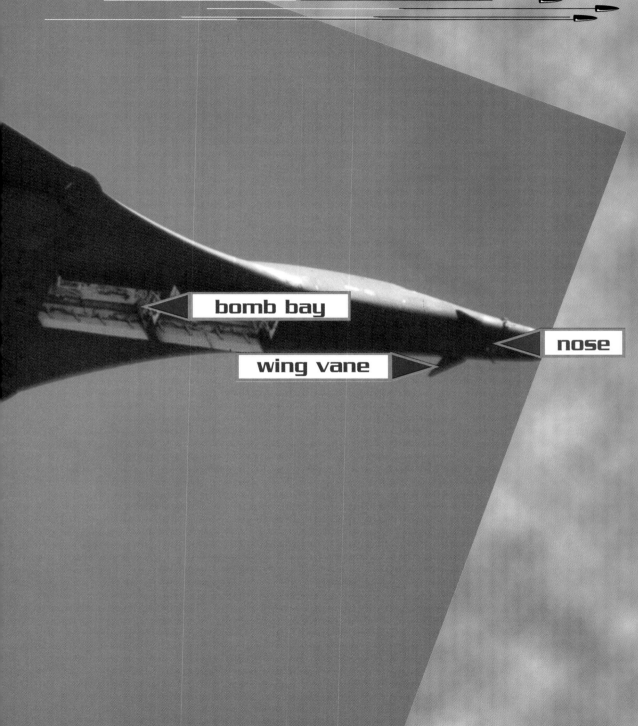

bomb bay

wing vane

nose

Chapter Three

Learn About

- B-1B bombs
- JDAMS
- Cluster bombs

Weapons and Tactics

The B-1B carries mainly air-to-ground weapons. It also can carry weapons to destroy enemy ships. The B-1B carries its weapons in three large storage areas called bomb bays. The bays are located near the center of the plane's body. The B-1B can carry about 75,000 pounds (34,020 kilograms) inside the bomb bays.

Some of the B-1B's bombs weigh 500 pounds.

Bombs

The B-1B often carries unguided bombs. These bombs are not guided by electronic systems.

The B-1B can carry 84 unguided bombs that each weigh 500 pounds (225 kilograms).

The B-1B also may carry 24 unguided bombs that each weigh 2,000 pounds (900 kilograms). Crew members use these bombs to destroy targets such as large buildings and bridges.

JDAMs

Crew members use Joint Direct Attack Missiles (JDAMs) when they cannot locate targets because of bad weather conditions. The JDAM includes a kit that fits over the tail of an unguided bomb. It adds a satellite receiver and a motor to the bomb.

Spacecraft called satellites orbit Earth and guide JDAMs. Satellite-guided weapons can accurately hit targets in bad weather conditions.

Other Weapons

The B-1B can carry up to 30 cluster bombs or CBU-97 Sensor Fuzed Weapons. Both types of bombs hold smaller bombs called submunitions. Smaller bombs can destroy targets spread out in a large area better than other bombs can.

A sensor explodes cluster bombs and CBU-97s as they fall over targets. The submunitions then drop from the bombs and explode when they hit an object. Each cluster bomb can release about 200 submunitions. A cluster bomb can affect an area about 700 by 1,300 feet (200 by 400 meters) wide. The CBU-97 releases 10 submunitions. Each CBU-97 can affect an area about 500 feet by 1,200 feet (150 by 370 meters) wide.

The B-1B can release Sensor Fuzed Weapons.

Chapter Four

Learn About

- Recent B-1B missions
- Improvements
- Future Air Force plans

The Future

Many people believe the B-1B is too expensive to operate. They believe the Air Force should retire it. The Air Force spends millions of dollars updating the planes. But many Air Force officials believe the B-1B is an important part of the military. Pilots have flown it on many successful missions. In 1999, B-1B crews took part in Operation Allied Force in southern Europe. Militaries involved in this operation wanted to force Yugoslavia's military out of a region called Kosovo.

In 2001, B-1B pilots performed missions during Operation Enduring Freedom. This operation targeted terrorists in the Middle Eastern country of Afghanistan. B-1B crews dropped more than 3 million pounds (1.4 million kilograms) of weapons during their missions.

Improvements

The Air Force often improves B-1Bs. In 1993, the Air Force began the Conventional

Mission Upgrade Program. The Air Force has improved the B-1B's communication, navigation, and radar jamming systems through this program.

In 2003, the Air Force plans to add a new towed decoy system to the B-1B. It will be called the AN/ALE-50.

New Bombs

Manufacturers are developing new bombs for the B-1B as part of the upgrade program. Raytheon is producing the satellite-guided AGM-154 Joint Standoff Weapon (JSOW) for the B-1B. The JSOW releases submunitions. It has a range of about 40 miles (64 kilometers).

The B-1B also will carry the Joint Air-to-Surface Standoff Missile (JASSM). Lockheed Martin is producing this missile. The JASSM has a range of about 1 mile (1.6 kilometers).

Air Force officials may soon retire some B-1Bs. But they plan to keep the bombers in service until about 2038. The Air Force depends on its B-1Bs to perform missions throughout the world.

Words to Know

chaff (CHAF)—strips of metal foil dropped by an aircraft to confuse enemy radar

drag (DRAG)—the force created when air strikes a moving object; drag slows down moving objects.

exhaust (eg-ZAWST)—heated air leaving a jet engine

radar (RAY-dar)—equipment that uses radio waves to locate and guide objects

submunition (sub-myoo-NI-shuhn)—a small bomb carried by a larger weapon and released as the weapon approaches its target

tanker (TANG-kur)—an airplane equipped with tanks for carrying liquids; tankers can refuel other planes during flight.

thrust (THRUHST)—the force created by a jet engine; thrust pushes an airplane forward.

To Learn More

Berliner, Don. *Stealth Fighters and Bombers.* Aircraft. Berkeley Heights, N.J.: Enslow, 2001.

Green, Michael. *The United States Air Force.* Serving Your Country. Mankato, Minn.: Capstone Press, 1998.

Sweetman, Bill. *Stealth Bombers: The B-2 Spirits.* War Planes. Mankato, Minn.: Capstone Press, 2001.

Useful Addresses

Air Combat Command
Office of Public Affairs
115 Thompson Street, Suite 211
Langley AFB, VA 23665

United States Air Force Museum
110 Spaatz Street
Wright-Patterson AFB, OH 45433

Internet Sites

Track down many sites about B-1B Bombers.
Visit the FACT HOUND at *http://www.facthound.com*

IT IS EASY!   IT IS FUN!

1) Go to *http://www.facthound.com*
2) Type in: 0736815082
3) Click on "FETCH IT" and FACT HOUND will find several links hand-picked by our editors.

Relax and let our pal FACT HOUND do the research for you!

Index